Day and Night and Other Dreams

PERFORMED BY

A Fine and Curious Company of Singers and Players

The Matanovic Family - Kathi, Milenko, Katya & Anya,
Nancy Rumbel, and Friends

Conceived by Cooper Edens for

GREEN TIGER PRESS

Published by Simon & Schuster

New York London Toronto Sydney Tokyo Singapore

GREEN TIGER PRESS
Simon & Schuster Building, Rockefeller Center
1230 Avenue of the Americas, New York, New York 10020.
Copyright © 1990 by Cooper Edens

GREEN TIGER PRESS is an imprint of Simon & Schuster.
Performed by A FINE & CURIOUS COMPANY
Published by permission of MUSIC FOR LITTLE PEOPLE
Manufactured in the United States of America

10   9   8   7   6   5   4   3   2

Library of Congress Cataloging-in-Publication Data
Day and night and other dreams / performed by A Fine and
Curious Company of Singers and Players (the Matanovic family—Kathi,
Milenko, Katya & Anya, Nancy Rumbel, and friends) ; conceived by
Cooper Edens for Green Tiger Press.   p.   cm.   Summary: An illustrated
collection of poems by Robert Louis Stevenson, William Blake,
Alfred, Lord Tennyson, and others.   Includes an audiocassette
of songs with lyrics from the poems.   1. Children's poetry,
English.   [1. English poetry—Collections.   2. Songs.]
I. Edens, Cooper.   II. Fine and Curious Company of Singers and Players.
[PR1175.3.D38   1991]   821.008'09282—dc20   91-3977   CIP
ISBN 0-671-75590-0

Illustration Credits:
Front cover by Carl Larsson
Frontispiece by Kate Greenaway
Title page by Jacynth Parsons
Copyright page by Margaret Ely Webb
Back cover by Jessie Willcox Smith

❧ CONTENTS ❧

PERFORMED BY
A Fine and Curious Company of Singers and Players

(The Matanovic family - Kathi, Milenko, Katya & Anya,
Nancy Rumbel, and Friends)

Milenko Matanovic - vocals, guitar, percussion, composing
Kathi Lightstone Matanovic - vocals
Katya Matanovic - vocals, composing
Anya Matanovic - vocals
Nancy Rumbel - oboe, English horn, ocarinas,
    cheng, percussion

Gladys Peto

Anonymous

Girls and Boys Come Out to Play

Girls and boys, come out to play,
The moon doth shine as bright as day,
Leave your supper and leave your sleep,
And come with your playfellows into the street.
Come with a whoop or come with a call,
Come with a goodwill or not at all.
Up the ladder and down the wall,
A halfpenny roll will serve us all.
You find milk and I'll find flour,
And we'll have a pudding in half an hour!

Anonymous

Margaret Ely Webb

Spring

Sound the flute!
Now it's mute.
Birds delight
Day and Night;
Nightingale
In the dale,
Lark in Sky,
Merrily, merrily, to welcome in the Year.

Little Boy,
Full of joy;
Little Girl,
Sweet and Small;
Cock does crow.
So do you;
Merry voice,
Infant noise,
Merrily, merrily, to welcome in the Year.

Little Lamb,
Here I am;
Come and lick
My white neck;
Let me pull
Your soft Wool;
Let me kiss
Your soft Face;
Merrily, merrily, to welcome in the Year.

William Blake

W. Graham Robertson

Somewhere

Could you tell me the way to Somewhere —
Somewhere, Somewhere,
I have heard of a place called Somewhere —
But know not where it can be.
It makes no difference,
Whether or not
I go in dreams
Or trudge on foot:
Would you tell me the way to Somewhere,
The Somewhere meant for me.

There's a little old house in Somewhere —
Somewhere, Somewhere,
A queer little house, with a Cat and a Mouse —
Just room enough for three.
A kitchen, a larder,
A bin for bread,
A string of candles,
Or stars instead,
A table, a chair,
And a four-post bed —
There's room for us all in Somewhere,
For the Cat and the Mouse and Me.

M. Boutet de Monvel

EMILY BENSON KNIPE

Anonymous

I want to be off to Somewhere,
To far, lone, lovely Somewhere,
I want to be off to Somewhere,
No matter where Somewhere be.
It makes no difference
Whether or not
I go in dreams
Or trudge on foot,
Or this time to-morrow
How far I've got,
Summer or Winter,
Cold, or hot,
Where, or When,
Or Why, or What —
Please, tell me the way to Somewhere —
Somewhere, Somewhere;
Somewhere, Somewhere, Somewhere, Somewhere —
The Somewhere meant for me!

Walter de la Mare

M. Boutet de Monvel

Maria L. Kirk

Where Go the Boats?

Dark brown is the river,
Golden is the sand.
It flows along for ever,
With trees on either hand.

Green leaves a-floating,
Castles of the foam,
Boats of mine a-boating—
Where will all come home?

On goes the river
And out past the mill,
Away down the valley,
Away down the hill.

Away down the river
A hundred miles or more,
Other little children
Shall bring my boats ashore.

Robert Louis Stevenson

Florence Edith Storer

Jessie Willcox Smith

My Shadow

I have a little shadow that goes in and out with me,
And what can be the use of him is more than I can see.
He is very, very like me from the heels up to the head;
And I see him jump before me, when I jump into my bed.

The funniest thing about him is the way he likes to grow—
Not at all like proper children, which is always very slow;
For he sometimes shoots up taller like an India-rubber ball,
And he sometimes gets so little that there's none of him at all.

He hasn't got a notion of how children ought to play,
And can only make a fool of me in every sort of way.
He stays so close beside me, he's a coward you can see;
I'd think shame to stick to nursie as that shadow sticks to me.

One morning, very early, before the sun was up,
I rose and found the shining dew on every buttercup;
But my lazy little shadow, like an arrant sleepyhead,
Had stayed at home behind me and was fast asleep in bed.

Robert Louis Stevenson

Charles Robinson

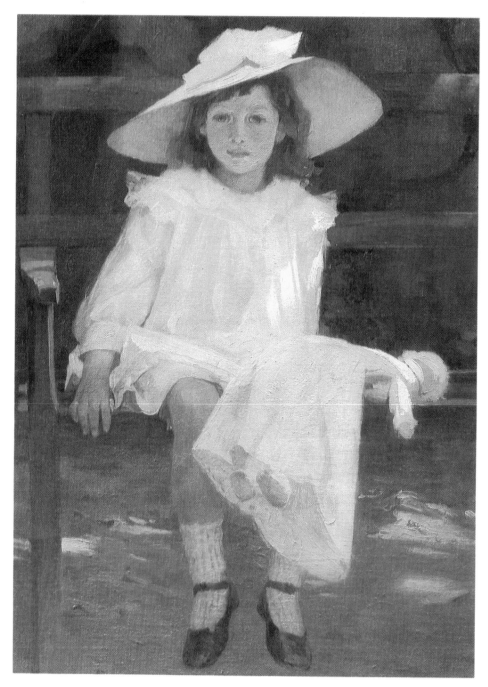

Alexander Mann

Little White Lily

Little white Lily
Sat by a stone,
Drooping and Waiting
Till the sun shone.
Little white Lily
Sunshine has fed;
Little white Lily
Is lifting her head.

Little white Lily
Said "It is good;
Little white Lily's
Clothing and food."
Little white Lily,
Drest like a bride!
Shining with whiteness,
And crown'd beside!

Little white Lily
Droopeth with pain,
Waiting and waiting
For the wet rain.
Little white Lily
Holdeth her cup;
Rain is fast falling
And filling it up.

Little white Lily
Said, "Good again,
When I am thirsty
To have nice rain;
Now I am stronger,
Now I am cool;
Heat cannot burn me,
My veins are so full!"

Little white Lily
Smells very sweet;
On her head sunshine,
Rain at her feet.
Thanks to the sunshine,
Thanks to the rain!
Little white Lily
Is happy again!

George MacDonald

General Store

Anonymous

Someday I'm going to have a store
With tinkly bells hung over the door,
With real glass cases and counters wide
And drawers all spilly with things inside.
There'll be a little of everything:
Bolts of calico, balls of string;
Jars of peppermint, tins of tea,
Potatoes and kettles and crockery;

Seeds in packets, scissors bright;
Kegs of sugar, brown and white;
Sarsaparilla for picnic lunches;
Bananas and rubber boots in bunches.
I'll fix the window and dust each shelf,
And take the money in all myself.
It will be my store and I will say:
"What can I do for you today?"

Rachel Field

The Peaceable Kingdom

Charles Robinson

Alligator, Beetle, Porcupine, Whale,
Bobolink, Panther, Dragonfly, Snail,
Crocodile, Monkey, Buffalo, Hare,
Dromedary, Leopard, Mud Turtle, Bear,
Elephant, Badger, Pelican, Ox,
Flying Fish, Reindeer, Anaconda, Fox,
Guinea Pig, Dolphin, Antelope, Goose,
Hummingbird, Weasel, Pickerel, Moose.
Ibex, Rhinoceros, Owl, Kangaroo,
Jackal, Opossum, Toad, Cockatoo,
Kingfisher, Peacock, Anteater, Bat,
Lizard, Ichneumon, Honeybee, Rat.
Mockingbird, Camel, Grasshopper, Mouse,
Nightingale, Spider, Octopus, Grouse,
Ocelot, Pheasant, Wolverine, Auk,
Periwinkle, Ermine, Katydid, Hawk.
Quail, Hippopotamus, Armadillo, Moth,
Rattlesnake, Lion, Woodpecker, Sloth,
Salamander, Goldfinch, Angleworm, Dog,
Tiger, Flamingo, Scorpion, Frog.
Unicorn, Ostrich, Nautilus, Mole,
Viper, Gorilla, Basilisk, Sole,
Whippoorwill, Beaver, Centipede, Fawn,
Xanthos, Canary, Polliwog, Swan.
Yellowhammer, Eagle, Hyena, Lark,
Zebra, Chameleon, Butterfly, Shark.

Traditional Shaker abecedarious

L. Leslie Brooke

The Throstle

"Summer is coming, summer is coming,
   I know it, I know it, I know it.
Light again, leaf again, life again, love again,"
   Yes, my wild little Poet.

Sing the new year in under the blue.
   Last year you sang it so gladly.
"New, new, new, new!" Is it then so new
   That you should carol so madly?

"Love again, song again, nest again, young again,"
   Never a prophet so crazy!
And hardly a daisy as yet, little friend,
   See, there is hardly a daisy.

"Here again, here, here, here, happy year!"
   O warble unchidden, unbidden!
Summer is coming, is coming, my dear.
   And all the winters are hidden.

Alfred, Lord Tennyson

Thomas Francis Dicksee

Honor C. Appleton

Clock-a-Clay

In the cowslip pips I lie
Hidden from the buzzing fly,
While green grass beneath me lies
Pearled wi' dew like fishes' eyes.
Here I lie, a clock-a-clay,
Waiting for the time o' day.

While grassy forests quake surprise,
And the wild wind sobs and sighs,
My gold home rocks as like to fall
On its pillar green and tall;
When the parting rain drives by
Clock-a-clay keeps warm and dry.

Day by day and night by night
All the week I hide from sight.
In the cowslip pips I lie,
In rain and dew still warm and dry.
Day and night, and night and day,
Red, black-spotted clock-a-clay.

My home it shakes in wind and showers,
Pale green pillar topped wi' flowers,
Bending at the wild wind's breath
Till I touch the grass beneath.
Here I live, lone clock-a-clay,
Watching for the time of day.

John Clare

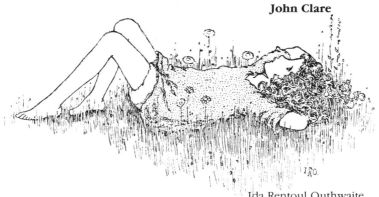

Ida Rentoul Outhwaite

I've Been Roaming

Anonymous

I've been roaming, I've been roaming,
  Where the meadow-dew is sweet,
And like a queen I'm coming
  With its pearls upon my feet.

I've been roaming, I've been roaming,
  O'er red rose and lily fair,
And like a sylph I'm coming
  With its blossoms in my hair.

I've been roaming, I've been roaming,
  Where the honeysuckle creeps,
And like a bee I'm coming
  With its kisses on my lips.

I've been roaming, I've been roaming,
  Over hill and over plain,
And like a bird I'm coming
  To my bower back again.

George Darley

Jessie Willcox Smith

Maria L. Kirk

A Swing Song

Swing, swing,
Sing, sing,
Here! my throne and I am a king!
   Swing, sing,
   Swing, sing,
   Farewell, earth, for I'm on the wing!

    Low, high,
    Here I fly,
    Like a bird through sunny sky;
       Free, free,
       Over the lea,
       Over the mountain, over the sea!

        Up, down,
        Up and down,
        Which is the way to London Town?
           Where? Where?
           Up in the air,
           Close your eyes and now you are there!

           Soon, soon,
           Afternoon,
           Over the sunset, over the moon;
              Far, far,
              Over all bar,
              Sweeping on from star to star!

              No, no,
              Low, low,
              Sweeping daisies with my toe.
                Slow, slow,
                To and fro,
                Slow_slow_
                slow_slow.

Ida Rentoul Outhwaite

William Allingham

Albertine Randal
Wheelan

Evening Song

Little Child, Good Child, go to sleep.
The tree-toads purr and the peepers peep
Under the apple-tree grass grows deep;
    Little Child, Good Child, go to sleep!

Big star out in the orange west;
Orioles swing in their Gypsy nest;
Soft wind singing what you love best;
    Rest till the sun-rise; rest, Child, rest!

Swift dreams swarm in a silver flight._
Hand in hand with the sleepy Night
Lie down soft with your eyelids tight._
    Hush, Child, little Child! Hush._ Goodnight._

Fannie Stearns Davis

S. Beatrice Pearce

Jessie Willcox Smith

Ida Rentoul Outhwaite

Lady Moon

"Lady Moon, Lady Moon, where are you roving?"
  "Over the Sea."
"Lady Moon, Lady Moon, whom are you loving?"
  "All that love me."
"Are you not tired with rolling, and never
Resting to sleep?
Why look so pale and so sad, as forever
Wishing to weep?"
  "Ask me not this, little child, if you love me:
  You are too bold;
  I must obey my dear Father above me,
  And do as I'm told."
"Lady Moon, Lady Moon, where are you roving?"
  "Over the Sea."
"Lady Moon, Lady Moon, whom are you loving?"
  "All that love me."

Lord Houghton

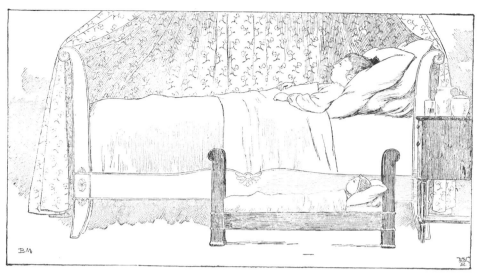

M. Boutet de Monvel

The Land of Nod

From breakfast on through all the day
At home among my friends I stay,
But every night I go abroad
Afar into the land of Nod.

All by myself I have to go,
With none to tell me what to do —
All alone beside the streams
And up the mountain-sides of dreams.

The strangest things are there for me
Both things to eat and things to see,
And many frightening sights abroad
Till morning in the land of Nod.

Try as I like to find the way,
I never can get back by day,
Nor can remember plain and clear
The curious music that I hear.

Robert Louis Stevenson

Margaret W. Tarrant

W. Graham Robertson

ANONYMOUS

Last Song

To the Sun
Who has shone
All day,
To the Moon
Who has gone
Away,
To the milk-white,
Silk-white,
Lily-white Star
A fond goodnight
Wherever you are.

James Guthrie

⊰ SONG CREDITS ⊱

Side 1 (23:24)

GIRLS AND BOYS COME OUT TO PLAY (3:13)***
Old Nursery Rhyme, music by Milenko Matanovic
Katya Matanovic and Anya Matanovic: vocals
Milenko Matanovic: vocals, guitar
Kathi Lightstone Matanovic: vocals
Patti Lightstone: vocals
Nancy Rumbel: double ocarina, oboe
Holly Miller: percussion

SPRING (3:05)**
Poem by William Blake, music by Katya Matanovic and Milenko Matanovic
Katya Matanovic and Anya Matanovic: vocals
Milenko Matanovic: vocals, guitar
Nancy Rumbel: double ocarina

SOMEWHERE (2:30)**
Poem by Walter de la Mare (excerpts), music by Milenko Matanovic
Anya Matanovic: vocals
Mike Correy: percussion, marimba
Nancy Rumbel: double ocarina
Milenko Matanovic: guitar

WHERE GO THE BOATS? (3:00)*
Poem by Robert Louis Stevenson, music by Milenko Matanovic
Kathi Lightstone Matanovic and Nancy Rumbel: vocals
Milenko Matanovic: guitar
Peter Reynolds: chimes

MY SHADOW (1:45)*
Poem by Robert Louis Stevenson, music by Nancy Rumbel
Bethany Ward: vocals
Nancy Rumbel: piano
Peter Reynolds: piano

LITTLE WHITE LILY (2:42)**
Poem by George MacDonald, music by Milenko Matanovic
Kathi Lightstone Matanovic: vocals
Katya Matanovic and Anya Matanovic: back-up vocals
Nancy Rumbel: double ocarina
Mike Correy: keyboard
Milenko Matanovic: guitar, back-up vocals

GENERAL STORE (1:47)*
Poem by Rachel Field, music by Katya Matanovic and Milenko Matanovic
Katya Matanovic: vocals
Nancy Rumbel: marimba
Milenko Matanovic: guitar
Peter Reynolds: synthesizer
Kathi Lightstone Matanovic: pots and glass bowls

THE PEACEABLE KINGDOM (4:40)*
Traditional Shaker abecedarious (the first letter in each line forms the alphabet), music by Milenko Matanovic
Bethany Ward, Katya Matanovic, Anya Matanovic, Kathi Lightstone Matanovic, David Edfeldt: vocals, whistles, general noises
Peter Reynolds: vocals, banjo, synthesizer
Nancy Rumbel: marimba and other assorted instruments
Lee Naasz: saxophone
Milenko Matanovic: vocals, guitar

Side 2 (23:24)

THE THROSTLE (2:58)***
Poem by Alfred, Lord Tennyson, music by Milenko Matanovic
Kathi Lightstone Matanovic, Katya Matanovic and Anya Matanovic: vocals
Milenko Matanovic: guitar, percussion, vocals
Nancy Rumbel: double ocarina, oboe, English horn
Holly Miller: percussion
Steve Boyce: percussion

CLOCK-A-CLAY (2:46)***
Poem by John Clare, music by Milenko Matanovic
Katya Matanovic: vocals
Kathi Lightstone Matanovic and Patti Lightstone: back-up vocals
Milenko Matanovic: guitar, back-up vocals, whistling
Nancy Rumbel: double ocarina, oboe, English horn

I'VE BEEN ROAMING (2:04)***
Poem by George Darley, music by Milenko Matanovic
Anya Matanovic and Katya Matanovic: vocals
Milenko Matanovic: guitar
Nancy Rumbel: double ocarina, oboe, English horn
Holly Miller: marimba

A SWING SONG (1:50)***
Poem by William Allingham, music by Milenko Matanovic
Anya Matanovic: vocals
Katya Matanovic: back-up vocals
Milenko Matanovic: guitar, marimba
Nancy Rumbel: oboe
Holly Miller: marimba

EVENING SONG (3:18)***
Poem by Fannie Stearns Davis, music by Milenko Matanovic
Kathi Lightstone Matanovic: vocals
Milenko Matanovic: guitar, percussion, vocals
Nancy Rumbel: English horn
Holly Miller: marimba

LADY MOON (3:04)**
Poem by Lord Houghton, music by Milenko Matanovic
Kathi Lightstone Matanovic, Katya Matanovic and Anya Matanovic: vocals
Milenko Matanovic: guitar, percussion, vocals
Nancy Rumbel: double ocarina, oboe, English horn

THE LAND OF NOD (4:55)*
Poem by Robert Louis Stevenson, music by Milenko Matanovic
Kathi Lightstone Matanovic: vocals
Milenko Matanovic: guitar, back-up vocals
Nancy Rumbel: cheng
Peter Reynolds and David Edfeldt: back-up vocals, bells

LAST SONG (1:57)**
Poem by James Guthrie, music by Milenko Matanovic
Kathi Lightstone Matanovic, Katya Matanovic, Anya Matanovic: vocals
Milenko Matanovic: vocals, guitar
Nancy Rumbel: cheng
Mike Correy: emax

---

* Recorded live by Brian Ziegler at Skysong, Issaquah, Washington, Summer 1987
** Recorded at JB Recordings, Jim Bachman engineer, Seattle, Washington, Spring 1989
*** Recorded by Steve Boyce, Kirkland, Washington, Autumn and Winter 1989

L. Hummel

The text of this book is set in Garamond Book
by So Cal Graphics of San Diego.

Calligraphed titles, cover, and interior design
by Judythe Sieck

Printing and binding
by Lake Book Manufacturing, Inc.,
Melrose Park, Illinois.